# Thank You

By buying this magazine, you support small business owners and small creators!

TalesOfTheGods aims to connect the metaphysical and spiritual communities.

Cover Photo - Owen Lee Heavenhill.

Everything in this magazine belongs to the contributor who submits it, anything that is not will be credited appropriately.

If you would like to write in anonymously, or join our team for the next edition feel free to send a email to TalesOTheGods@gmail.com

TalesOfTheGods, March 2021

facebook.com/groups/665578877692886

# Contributors

| | |
|---|---|
| Desirée Goulden | Owner, layout design, contributor |
| Owen Lee Heavenhill | Photographer, Contributor |
| Dana Lee Beaudreau | Founding member, Contributor |
| Veronica | Founding member, Contributor |

The TalesOfTheGods & Practical Witchcraft magazine is a community project. Our roster of contributors is constantly shifting. Everyone who works on the magazine takes home an equal take of the income from the sales of this magazine.

We aim to bring education and entertainment to people of all levels of experience and paths. If you have a point of view that you would like to share with the world, feel free to reach out to join us. We are currently looking for people of colour to join us. Whether you are a teacher, or just interested in taking part, we have a place for you.

Have a shop or product you want to share with the world? Contact us and we will run a free full page ad for you in the next edition! We release on every day of the wheel of the year, so it's easy to follow release dates!

We understand that there may be some who may not want to support Amazon, so we have made the shift from publishing through Kindle Direct Publishing for our paper back editions to Ingram Spark. This will allow for wider distribution (Chapters, Barns & Noble, indie book shops) for those who want to support us without supporting Amazon and Jeff Bezos.

**Please know that all opinions are that of the contributor and may not reflect the team in general.**

# Contents

| | |
|---|---|
| About Lughnasadh | PAGE 2 |
| To the exhausted witch - Poem by Owen | PAGE 4 |
| Photography showcase | PAGE 5 |
| Preserving The Past & Future | PAGE 8 |
| All About Sage | PAGE 12 |
| Modern Ethics In The Online Pagan World | PAGE 14 |
| Crosswords | PAGE 20 |
| The Sigils Of Hermes Divination Intro | PAGE 25 |
| Restraining Order Because You're Wiccan *Reprint | PAGE 30 |

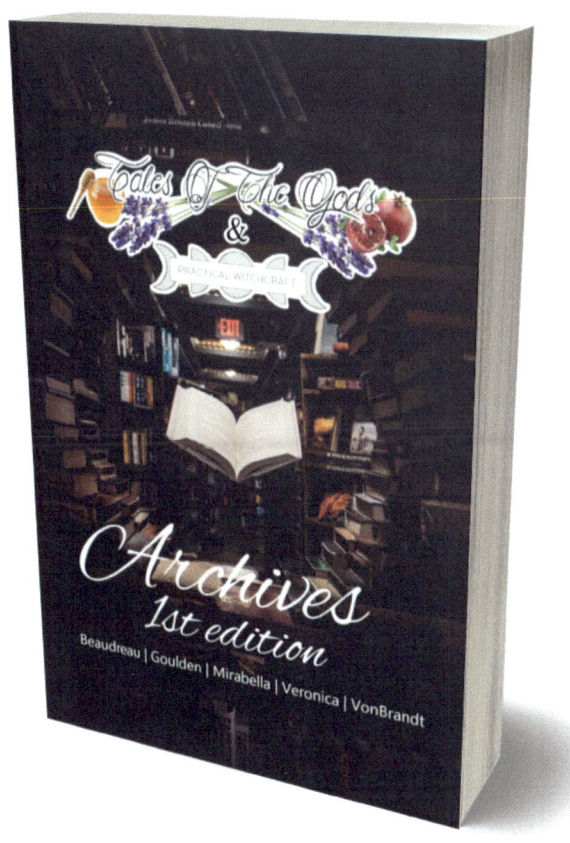

Want to read the articles of the magazine, but have visual setbacks with the magazine format? Want to read without having the budget to buy every magazine?
The Archives are all of our articles in plain text format for your bookcase or digital collection!
Published every 3 magazine editions this has a plethora of knowledge and entertainment!
31 articles, 201 pages of content, all for an affordable price! ($20 cad)
https://www.talesofthegods.com/magazine

Lughnasadh

Lughnasadh is the 6th day on the Wheel Of The Year. Taken from Irish Gaelic religion, it celebrates the deity Lugh and his foster mother, Tailtiu.

It is an agricultural celebration and is said that Lugh created the holiday his self for Tailtiu who died while clearing the fields of Ireland for agriculture.

I is sometimes also called Lammas in the Anglo-Saxon world, and within medieval England and Scotland and is named for the loaf-mass where the first loaf of bread is consecrated. It also may have become known as the "Feast of the First Fruits" and was a time to give thanks for divine gifts.

Lughnasadh is traditionally celebrated on a hill or mountain top with an alter pointed to the west to represent autumn.

Co-relations and symbology:

**Colours**

**Gold, Yellow, Orange, Brown ,Green**

**Symbols**

**Corn, Wheat, Bread, Sun Symbols, Lugh's Spear**

 The Underworld Oracle Deck
By Desiree Goulden

25 Full colour cards

Works with reversed cards

Works with other decks

$23.99 Cad

https://www.thegamecrafter.com/games/the-underworld-oracle-deck

## Owen Lee Heavenhill

## Contributor / Photographer

# What Are Influencers?

When doing a reading for a client, often you may feel you need further clarification. Whether you use Tarot, Cartomancy, Palmistry, Numerology, Astrology, Phrenology, Kirlian Photography, Runes, Ogham, or any other method, there will be times where what comes to you is not always clear. At such times it may be necessary to consult other reading materials.

An influencer is described as one to three cards from another source that help to explain what is before you in your initial reading. Often the reader will choose to use Angel cards, Oracle cards, Spirit cards, or any other card of choosing, dependant on the reader's background. (As a Christian Witch and a Metis descendant, I often choose to use Spirit cards or Angel cards.)

The idea behind the influencer card is to streamline your reading. From you will meet someone new, you may see that the individual is not all that he seems to be or that he holds ill intent and to give your client a heads up is better than to send a sheep off into the hills alone to face the wolves.
How to use an influencer?

Begin by doing your intended reading. Look over how it all fits together and not just the individual components. What story does this portray? Is there any underlying issue that it appears they are not dealing with or unwilling to face? If so, you may want to look closer. Ask the subject to select an influencer card or three. First examine the card(s) on there own. What do they signify or what is their accepted meaning?

Then look again at how this works if added to the reading. Place the influencer on your spread where you feel it belongs and consider how this changes the reading, in part or in whole.
It is also possible to use an influencer in absence of a reading. Many psychic/intuitive/empathic readers will draw a card at the start of the day to see how their day may be influenced. In this case, everyone has their own preference as to what method speaks most clearly to them.

One of the more common/popular influencer cards is The Crow. This majestic and familiar bird holds great affinity for many of us as friend or familiar. As watchful and resourceful creatures, these birds represent transformation and change. When the crow card appears, know that you need to be more alert to what is going on around you and how the people and circumstances around you are influencing you. You may not be prepared to face the things that are about to arrive on the scene, but you need to know that you are strong enough to face them, to get through them and that, like the crow collects objects into its nest, you have all the tools that you need. All resources you require will be provided, much as the crow is able to forage for all of its life requirements.

(Disclaimer: This card is from the Spirit Animal deck and its reading comes from my grandmother's teaching as a Ojibway descendant.)

*-Dana Lee Beaudreau*

# Preserving The Past & Future

Our legacy is what we leave behind. The art, structures, religion, environment, and culture that we leave behind will be what future generations judge us by.

The Ancients left us their monuments, temples, buried cities, art, and living religions as a reminder of their great civilizations. We can go to the sites of these old places and connect and learn from those who came before. These remains have stood the test of time... until now.

In 2021 many pagan and historical sites have been put in danger by their governments in the name of "development"

Take for example, the many ancient temples and remains in Greece. As a major source of tourism and income in a country that has been dealing with a Government Debt Crisis since the global financial crisis of 2007-8, it is understandable that the Greek government would funnel money into the preservation and renovation of these sites.

The temple of Apollo Epicurius in Bassae was made in 420 BCE and is a a combination of Doric, Ionic, and Corinthian style architecture. The Corinthian style of ancient Greek pillars and architecture being widely lost to history after being looted by British archaeologists and then lost at sea in the 1900s.

It survived for thousands of years before the Greek government in 1986 decided to cover it completely to "preserve it from winds and acid rain" (A thing that surely were it a problem, would have taken its toll in the thousands of years since it's building.) with a large white tarp. The intent was to rebuild and renovate the already well preserved temple but nothing ever came of it and the project was dropped after the recession. Thus, the beauty of the temple was replaced with a eyesore of a tarp that arguably was not needed.

This is not a stand alone problem within Greece either. The Parthenon is a extremely popular tourist spot in Athens and has been under some sort of reconstruction and preservation for some time now, but recently due to "...poor planning, political pressure to hastily complete a dangerous and destructive renovation" (kosmodromio.gr) it has flooded for the first time in 2500 years. The government pushed for an extensive paved road through the premises for "accessibility" and "connivance".

Things like this is not exclusive to Greece, however. Stonehenge, a notorious pagan monument and site, located in Wiltshire, England, is now in danger of losing it's World Heritage Site title. It is in danger of losing it's status, because a $2.3 billion highway tunnel is planned to be built near the site. If the highway is built as planned, and Stonehenge loses it's status, it will also lose it's protection as a World Heritage Site, leaving it open for the government, developers, and the highest bidder to decide what happens to it.

It is not only places from the past that are at risk by the short sighted need for capitol and development, however. It is also the land of the future.

The native Anishinaabe water protectors are fighting against Enbridge pipeline 3. Line 3 cuts through untouched Anishinabbe treaty wetlands, through the Mississippi river, and the shore of Lake Superior. (The largest freshwater source in not only Canada, but the world). The pipeline puts in danger fresh water sources, the majority of wild rice sources, (a major food sourced for the widely disenfranchised native peoples of Turtle Island / Canada, the USA.) and sacred grounds. It is planned to be completed by the

- end of this year, despite the current legal battle and protests against it.

If this sounds familiar, it's because it happens a lot. This happened with the Standing Rock pipeline, which was eventually stopped by President Barack Obama... and then allowed the moment Trump took office. The natives of Standing Rock Sioux Tribe fought against the pipeline, facing extreme violence at the hands of the police. Just like the Anishinaabe are now. They spoke of a destructive entity called the Black Snake that represents destruction and bares a likeness to oil spills. They warned that the Standing Rock Keystone pipeline would leak, and it was a matter of "when" not "if".

They were proven right in October 2019 when the Keystone pipe leaked and caused one of the largest spills in North Dakota, spilling 383,000 gallons of crude oil in the surrounding wetlands.

We as a species need to start to learn to consider time. The unfortunate reality is that money hungry people and leaders refuse to see anything beyond the present. We need to preserve the cultures and structures of the past. We need to acknowledge that they have stood the test of time and that do not always need our modern "improvements". We need to look to and preserve the future as well as the past. We can not allow our wetlands, and native sites and land to be polluted and destroyed by big oil. (A energy source that is quickly being out paced by green energy.)

We stand at a turning point in time. The reality of our actions are now becoming evident and must be addressed. The Parthenon has already been paved, nothing can be done there. The temple of Apollo is fine, even if it is an eyesore now. Stonehenge has recently won their fight against losing it's title and the tunnel being built. The Anishinaabe have had no such luck. Faced with RCMP and private hired police violence, Enbridge ignoring their protests and paying law

The water protectors need your support. The links below are petitions you can sign, and places to donate to protect the water and the native peoples who's food and sacred land is in danger.

https://www.stopline3.org/take-action

https://www.honorearth.org/stop_line_3

https://mn350.org/campaigns/stop-line-3-pipeline/

https://stopthemoneypipeline.com/line3/

*-Desirée Goulden*

# All About Sage

### What is Sage?

Also known as Salvia Flower, sage grows in summer to autumn in sunny well-drained areas.
Part of the mint family, these plants grow tall with square flowers and velvety leaves.  Good for the planet, they attract hummingbirds, butterflies, and bees to the region.  They also work to repel deer, rabbits, small animals, and other garden pests.
While there are many different kinds of sage and every type has its own uses, traditionally, sage is used by many of the arts for cleansing evil or dark chi from the area where practitioners have been assisting their subjects.

### Types of Sage

The most commonly types of sage used by witches would be common white sage (used for smudging, sometimes combined with lavender or mint), garden sage is most commonly used for brewing a tea used to enhance memory, Pineapple sage which can be brewed to make an antibacterial medicine, Clary sage is used as an eye bath in order to enforce clarity of vision.  According to many sources online, there are potentially over 700 different types of Sage.

### The Many Uses of Sage

Over history, sage has been used for many purposes.  The most commonly acknowledged these days is that of a purifier, whether through sage sticks, incense, or a tea infusion (when trying to purify the person from the inside).  It has also been used in cooking, and while we all believe that this is for the lovely taste it adds to our food, the root of this practice comes from the beliefs that medicinally, when consumed, sage could heal a damaged or sick liver.

Sage was also associated with wealth. The more sage a person grew in their garden the wealthier the household was believed to be. A bath of the leaves infused with lavender was believed to reduce fever, calm anxiety and agitation, and to enhance a person's visionary powers. It is also believed that a person bathing in sage and rosemary would enhance their life and add to their longevity. When stirred in wine, can be used against cramps and side stitches caused by gas.

Harvesting Your Sage

Never use iron or steel tools in harvesting your sage. Also, sage pushes forth best if it is harvested in full moonlight. Some forms of sage are perennials and taking care of your harvesting ensures a good crop from year to year.

Preparations for Sage

Do not limit yourself in the possible applications of sage. Sage can be made into a bath, a tea, a smudge stick, an amulet, a potion, a poultice, a cooking herb, or an essential oil.

Warning: Too much consumption of the sage oil, not essential oil, will lead to a feeling of nausea that can be confused with intoxication.

*-Dana Lee Beaudreau*

# Modern ethics in the online occult & spiritual communities.

(Note, this is from my experience online and contains dark content as well as personal opinions )

The 2020s has brought a wave of social awareness and justice in all walks of life. The occult and spiritual communities in particular.

Many of the magical practices we share today have similarities or are borrowed from other practices. As such, we should all pay attention and be active in the attempt to learn and replace practices and terminology that takes from or negatively effects a minority or closed demographic / practice / religion.

These will be some small explanations for newer notions that many may not know about if they are not present in the online sphere of the occult & paganism. Some may have even been common place in your practices for some time, so here are some practices and terms that may land you in hot water online for doing / saying.

Please note that everyone has their own ethics and views on things and many of these comes down to ones personal values and views. This is by no means a "IF YOU DO THIS YOU ARE EVIL" list, this is only to help people while interacting with the wider occult and pagan communities in a respectful manner.

Blessings Without Permission

While one may think that receiving blessings and beneficial workings would always be good, this is not always the case. It is always best to seek the permission of the person you are blessing. Failing to do so at best can be just uncomfortable.

It's like being told by a Christian that they will pray for you. It may be a kindness in their eyes, but unless you are part of their religion it can be awkward at best. At worst, it can be a notion from a religion your own religion or personal beliefs come in conflict with. This can go for all walks and paths. Not every religion has had a happy past with others.

It can also bring up problems with your deities if you have a close working relationship with them or worship of them. If someone tries to bless you invoking the name of a deity that is in direct conflict with your own deity it could back fire on the person you are trying to bless, or yourself.

Blessings and beneficial workings can be a kindness, but it would be best for you to touch base with the person you're trying to work on so that you don't step on anyone's toes or make things awkward.

Claiming Unearned Titles

Titles can show your experience in situations wherein it is relevant. Unfortunately, many people see them as a way to get clout online.

For most titles, there are years of experience you need, a person to bestow the title upon you, prerequisites to meet, and people to validate that you are who and what you claim to be. You can not just decide that calling yourself a Priestess would look good for your image and proclaim to the world that you are a Priestess, and should be treated as such. That's not how that works, and it's a great way to be laughed at by actual officials of whatever order you are claiming to be clergy for.

This isn't just for the title of Priestess, there are those who are claiming that they are Crones and Elders online because they are older that others in their online or offline social circle... while being 30 with less than 6 years of experience. Being the oldest in your social circle does not a Crone or Elder make. You can not claim these titles arbitrarily whilst having less experience than most 19-year-olds. It takes away from the weight that these titles carry and thus the validity of actual Crones and Elders. To put it in perspective, you wouldn't walk into a retirement home of military vets and demand the same respect they are given because "I'm a 90 year old vet too!" while obviously being a 35 year old librarian.

Closing Open Practices

This seems to be a phenomenon I have seen exclusively online by well meaning younger people trying to be socially aware without really doing much to look into what they are looking at.

People have tried to claim that tarot cards are a closed practice belonging only to the Romani people... Despite the Romani people saying that's false, and that Tarot can be traced back to a card game in Italy and France, known as  trionfi, tarocchi ,tarock, an eventually tarot. It is said that standard playing cards are based off them originally.

While closed or marginalized practices and peoples may incorporate certain objects, or have similar practices that does not mean that that is the only correct version, and everything else is stolen from them. Humanity and it's cultures are not so unique as we often think and there are many similarities between practices.

You can acknowledge that there are similarities but jumping to claiming that something is stolen without the proper research, while ignoring the people from the practice that you're trying to close saying that you're wrong isn't doing what you think it is. It may actively make people take actual closed practices less seriously as they assume that is just another kid online trying to get social justice brownie points.

Gypsy

This is a term we all know to describe the travelling Romani peoples. There are however a growing population of Romani people within the USA and Canada who have started to speak up against the term "Gypsy".

For a background, the Romani people are a Indo-Aryan peoples who traditionally are nomadic. They live throughout Europe, and the diaspora live within the Americas. A major aspect of their history is their enslavement at the hands of present day Romania which they endured from the years of 1241 to the 1850s. (Roughly 600 years.)

Within Czechoslovakia starting in 1973 forced sterilizations have been forced upon Romani women which while no longer policy, still exists in high levels of coerced sterilization of Romani women.

Throughout the world, the Roma populations deal with their encampments being destroyed, high levels of poverty, low

- levels of education and educational opportunities, and high levels of employment discrimination,

The English word for the Romani people is Gypsy and has become a point of contention in the west. The west has a peculiar relationship with the Roma people.

We in the west still see them as thieves, creating terms like "gypped" to explain if you've been scammed or stolen from. We still see them as uneducated, impoverished, travellers and even though we have not had the history with them that Romania has, they still deal with a lot of prejudice in the west.

While we cast them in this negative life, we somehow still idolize a romanticized version of their life. We promote the "traveller" and "boho" lifestyle, taking influence from Roma traditions, fashions, etc and profiting off the white washed and polished version of them. While we use them to bring in profit in the form of fashion, music, lifestyle blogs and influencers, the actual Roma people deal with the same low quality of life as they have endured elsewhere in the world. We profit from shows like "My Big Fat Gypsy Wedding" and laugh and mock their society while funnelling money into white TV show runners.

We actively equate "Travellers" and "Boho" with whiteness and money, while the people we based and take these notions from as "Gypsy" "Thieves" "Stupid" "Dirty". These are very particular problems within western society that is specific to the Romani experience in Canada and The US. While Gypsy was originally just the English term for Romani, we have turned it into a slur, and the Romani people have seen and voiced that.

There are growing waves of Romani groups who take the term "Gypsy" as a slur and it makes sense, because that's exactly how we have been using the term as. There are people across seas who proclaim that "It's just the English term, and it's not a slur you westerners are insane and obsessed with oppression."… while refusing to acknowledge that a American Romani person faces completely different challenges and realities of oppression than a Romani person from England. There are people who have grown up calling Romani people "Gypsies" and claim that "That's just what they're called" while ignoring the Roma people who try to explain why that word has evolved as words always to in the ever changing English language. There are also Romani people in the west who disagree with the idea that it's a slur.

No matter your ideas of the word, many people are telling you that it is a slur that has negative connotations that harms the people you say it to. When someone tells you something hurts them, it is never your place to say "no it doesn't." Roma people from the west are asking that in western dominated spaces that you use the word "Roma" rather than "Gypsy" and while this segment may seem long and preachy, it's length is only trying to explain why they feel this way. We should all work to make the world a more comfortable place for everyone and attempt to listen to people who we unintentionally hurt without claiming that they are wrong.

Love Spells

Good ol' love spells. One of the first thing people think about when they think of Witches. Love spells have gotten a lot of flack recently with the new waves of young practitioners coming into the craft.

There is the false idea that doing a love spell on someone is exactly the same as drugging and raping them and that consent can never be given under a love spell. This is over estimating the effects of a love spell. People can give consent under them, but there are still very dangerous aspects to love spells.

People under love spells (or at least improperly done love spells where in the other person is not privy to it being done.) have a tenancy for being violently obsessive. These people very quickly turn to stalking, harming others to get the person who they were worked on to love, not being able to think or focus of anything else, obsessive dreams about the person they were made to want for. In some cases if this goes too far it is not uncommon for them to meet violent and deadly ends.

Love spells can be very effective ways to build on a existing relationship between two consenting partners utilizing a experienced practitioner who knows how to properly do the working. People in general look down upon doing love spells in general, but particularly on an unwilling and unknowing partner.

Rule Of Three

You'd be hard pressed to meet a practitioner or pagan who doesn't know about the Rule Of Three. A major tenant of Neo-Wiccan tradition, it states that everything you do will return to you in 3's and "An do as ye wilt if it harms none." Unfortunately this very useful general rule has been weaponized by some people much in the same way as sin and hell has been weaponized by the Christians

- against magical practices they disagree with.

Wicca is very much credited with bringing both the occult and paganism to the west, but that does not make Wicca the moral ruler of all magick. Not every witch is Wiccan, so when you come onto a post of a person doing a baneful working, and comment about how they "need to adhere to the 3 fold law." it doesn't reflect well upon yourself. Your morals are not everyone else's morals. Your religion isn't everyone else's religion. If you would not take well to a Christian telling you you are going to burn in hell for being Wiccan, you should not then turn to people doing baneful workings and tell them to follow the 3 fold law or they will be punished by karma. We get what we give, yes, so by that notion we should give respect for practices that are not our own.

### Smudging

Smudging is part of closed native practices. Unless you are a native from the west, you can not and likely have no idea how to properly smudge. You are looking for the term "smoke cleansing."

While smudging is part of native practice (native religion and practices within the west being illegal until 1851 in Canada and 1978 in the USA) and incorporates sacred medicine, prayer, and tools that we have no claim to as the peoples who have made them illegal, and attempted to wipe out through systematic oppression and a attempted cultural genocide.

Smoke cleansing exists across the world in nearly every practice and you can pull from them to smoke cleanse more effectively than attempting to cleanse by smudging without knowing how to do so, and frustrating the native spirits who observe you as you do this.

### Speaking For Gods

We have many ways to speak to divinity. Through mediums, divination, observation of the natural world, many are in contact and receive messages from their deities. That being said, you being able to get these messages does not mean you speak for the gods.

If someone is doing something or saying something that you dislike, it will never be your place to claim that "God(dess) XYZ said you're wrong and evil and they hate you!". I is a best distasteful, at worst a bold display of hubris which can put you at odds with your community and the deity in question.

- If a deity dislikes something, they will let the person know directly themselves, not through a strangers tarot, oracle, or runes.

### Spirit Animal

Another native term which have very significance religious value exclusive to native people and tribes in the west. While some form of spiritual animal guides have existed in some cultures across time ( in Greek; spiritus animalis in Latin, etc) the Spirit Animals of native practice are different and part of a marginalized and previously illegal religious practice.

While some claim that they are practising Italian magic and that's the English word, I personally believe that if they were actually practising Italian magic and referring to Italian spirit animals, they would say the Italian word. People do have animal spirit guides, and if that is to what you are referring to, then they can be called animal guides as not to infringe on the native practices. If you are claiming you are using the native spirit animals while not being native or part of any tribe and have not gone through the proper channels, you are either mistaken or wrongfully practising a closed practice.

### Spiritual Bypassing

"The mundane over the magical." No amount of magical prowess, or spiritual belief comes before medical science. If you or (as in most cases) your child are feeling different to others. If you don't connect with people, feel what you perceive to be "too much" or "not enough" then you need to seek out a doctor. Everyone wants to feel special and many are afraid of certain medical labels, but ignoring them and applying spiritual terminology while posting dangerous information online harms yourself and others.

There is no shame in a medical diagnoses. There is shame in ignoring your mental and physical health and actively convincing others to do so because of some magickal or mythical reason with little real evidence.

### UPG As Gospel

Unverified personal gnosis is not absolute truth. People experience everything from their particular perspective. We all look to the same sky and see different shades of blue. Just because you see things one way, doesn't make it the only way. I may personally believe that Ares has brown eyes, but it is not my place to attack

- those who would claim that he has blue. Just because you may experience something, it does not mean that you should attack or go after others who have not experience that same thing.

### White Sage

White Sage is part of native smudging rituals and is a sacred medicine which is endangered in the Americas. Unless you are part of the native communities, it is destructive to buy White Sage which is sold by white retailers. The herb is endangered and should be available to the natives who's religion it belongs to, and if money is to be made off it, it should be money in the pockets of the natives who are not afforded the same opportunities as the rest of us.

There are about 600 species of sage, and you can buy common sage for less at Bulk Barn, Target, Walmart, and most grocery stores.

*—Desirée Goulden*

# Metaphysical Crossword!

Answers in back of publication.

1- A nature based religion created in the 1900s.
2- The religion of the Ancient Greeks.
3- The people, and religion that is known as the Vikings.
4- A profession, not a people.
5- A non-Abrahamic religion.
6- One who sees the future.
7- An alphabet and divination tool.
8- Answers yes no and maybe questions.
9- God who created the Norse runes.
10- Father of Hermes whose epithet is Xenios

# The Future, Regrettably
## Coming Fall 2021

The debut urban fantasy novel from Desirée Goulden, prequel to the Aurora Garroway series.

Julian is a man with nothing but a name. Woken from a coma and thrust into a war he does not want to fight, he is the body guard and right hand man of a tyrannical cult leader, Rose. Escape is futile and attempts cause innocent people to be killed to keep him in line. With death as the only escape, he becomes reckless in battle, hoping to be cut down and finally escape the life he is trapped in.

Rose notices and offers him a boon: stay in line and do as she says and he will be able to visit the future in his dreams. He will be able to live a comfortable life and see why the Conduit Hierarchy's war is just, and how it will better the world.

Will this be enough to pacify Julian? Or will this motivate him to tear down the organization that seeks to control him, and find the truth?

# Olympian Crossword!

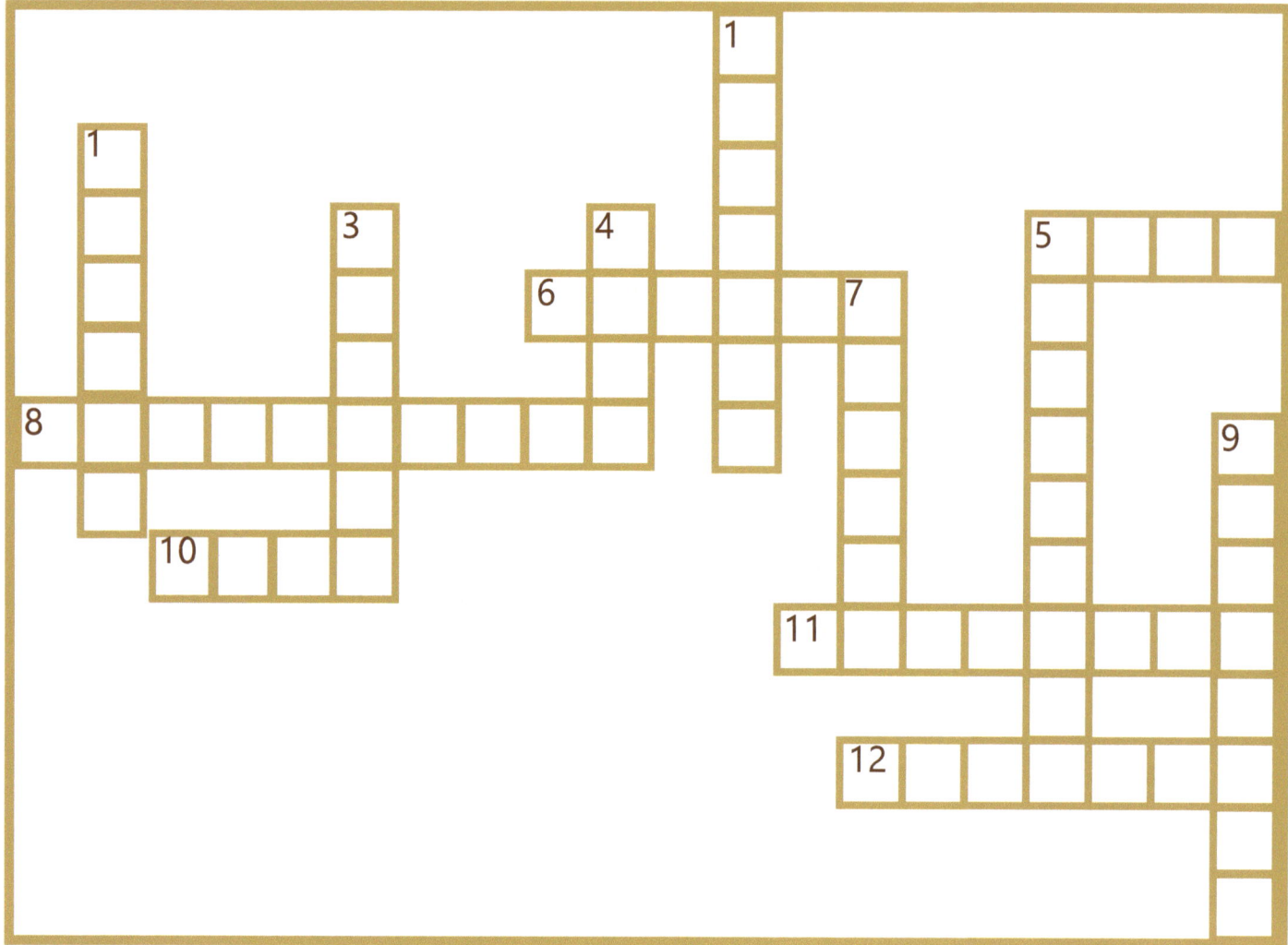

Answers in back of publication.

Across

5. God of civil order and battle lust.
6. A former Olympian
8. Creator of Talos.
10. Competed against Aphrodite and Athena for the golden apple.
11. God of earthquakes
12. Goddess of childbirth protector of girls.

Down

1. Goddess of agriculture.
2. Creator of the lyre.
3. Goddess of good wisdom.
4. God of kings and fate.
5. Loved Adonis.
7. God of archery and plague.
9. Reborn Zagrus .

# Crystal Crossword!

Answers in back of publication.

Across
3. range of colours and crystal tends to be highly fluorescent under UV light
5. a set of closely related minerals forming a group whose stone comes in many vibrant colours
7. strontium based crystal
9. A purple variety of quartz
10. commonly associated with malachite and has deep blue colouring

Down
1. dark green, copper-based mineral
2. uncommon stone. vibrant, pink to rose red colored mineral
4. naturally formed as smoky quartz is slowly heated inside the earth
6. most common type of crystal
8. Fools Gold

# Introduction To The Sigils Of Hermes

Since finding out I am a medium, there is little I have actually done with the gift beyond personal deity communication. Partially from being socially awkward, and partially because a deep fear of being judged. I've kept my abilities to myself and gone about my life... that was until I released the Underworld Oracle Deck.

The moment I began that project, Hermes (a god I worship and work with closely) took immediate interest. He kept an eye on my progress and made remarks about runes, divination in general, and the affordability of most divination tools. I made a one off comment about how most divination tools are pricey, and those that aren't are not accessible to people living in the brook closet. He told me that I should "figure out a solution to that" and I laughed it off.

Hermes, however, did not. Apparently to Hermes "You should figure out a solution to that." means, "you are going to do intense guided meditation with me to access your akashic records in conjunction with my input and help to create a new divination system, and you're going to like it." While the hand guide and sets are not yet finished, here is a sneak peak of the project and a brief explanation of the sigils.

The sigils of Hermes are 12 sigils connected to the zodiac and created by Hermes with the aid of a human scribe. These sigils can be used in divination, as well as spellwork of all kinds, much like the Norse Eldar Futhark runes. For accessibility the Sigils of Hermes can be created by anybody and come in 3 forms for covert and affordable options. These are made with affordability and people who are in the boom closet in mind, as they were created when I myself was homeless and in a place where divination tools would be looked at poorly.

The first form of the sigils comes in the form of playing dice. Take 2 dice of different colours and on each side of the faces of the die, put a mark to denote the "bottom" of the sigil. Herme's sigils are read in 4s, roll the pair of dice twice get the full reading and record the results. Alternitavely, if you have a 12 sided die roll it 4 times. (If you have a 12 sided die, we know you are a DnD nerd and have more, you may chose to just roll 4 of them.) If you get a repeat sigil, reroll the last.

The second form are tiles or stones. Take a permanent marker and mark your tiles or stones with the sigils and toss to read them. The 4 that stand apart from the tossed pile are the 4 for your reading.

The third form are playing cards or oracle cards. If you have blank cards of some sort, simply draw the sigils on, shuffle and pull 4. If you have a standard playing deck, remove the king cards and shuffle. Numbers are as ordered with Ace being 1- Movement, Jack being 11- The Summit, and Queen being 12- The Bolt Of Zeus. Shuffle and pull discarding duplicates.

1-Movement.
Action, life, the possibility of growth and new beginnings. Associated with Aries.
Reverse: Stop, stalemate, death, endings.

2-Push.
Movement, force, effort, drive to succeed, initialization. Associated with Taurus.
Reverse: Obstacles, lack of energy, apathy.

3-Block.
Stops, setbacks, blocking, protection. Associated with Gemini.
Reverse: Continuations, breaking down of protections, overstepped boundaries, danger.

4-Lance.
Power, force, action, focused attack, damage. Associated with Cancer.
Reverse: half-hearted, ineffective, weak willed, failed attack or approach.

5-Oar.
Support, guidance, teamwork, leadership. Associated with Leo
Reverse: Working alone, follower mentality, lack of support, stubbornness.

6-Radiance.
Hope, positivity, victory, earned knowledge, self confidence. Associated with Virgo.
Reverse: Self-consciousness, disrepair, depression, ignorance.

7-The Shield.
Protection, safety, community, family. Associated with Libra.
Reverse: Isolation, broken family, broken relationships, vulnerability.

8-The All Seeing Eye.
Divine oversight, being watched, being seen, clarity. Associated with Scorpio.
Reverse: Hidden, Unknown, confusion, sneaky.

9-The Serpent.
Fertility, strength, nature, haste. Associated with Sagittarius.
Reverse: Weakness, barren, sloth.

10-The Spiraling Star
Journey, soul journey, learning, expanding, the spirit, human imperfections, uniqueness. Associated with Capricorn.
Reverse: Artificial perfection, copycat, dead ends, willful ignorance.

11-The Summit.
Peak of power, the highest point, authority, ability, royalty, a steady base. Associated with Aquarius.
Reverse: Rock bottom, no stability, lack of authority, ineptitude.

**12-The Bolt Of Zeus.**

Destructive power, removing obstacles, destroying what held you back, ascension to power. Associated with Pisces.

Reverse: Held back, fall from grace, self-destruction, obstacles.

Keep an eye out for the official handbook with more in depth information and interpretations, as well as official dice, card, and tile sets! More information to come on TalesOfTheGods.com and the TalesOfTheGods & Practical Witchcraft Magazine. If you use the Sigils of Hermes, let us know! Tag them with #sigilsofhermes on TikTok, Instagram, Twitter, and Tumblr and let us know what you think!

*-Desirée Goulden*

# Jim Two Snakes
# Spiritual Advisor

 facebook.com/jimtwosnakes

 instagram.com/jimtwosnakes

 patreon.com/spiritualdad

Many people think the term Spirituality is about religion, but it doesn't have to be. In fact I think most people are Spiritual no matter if they are religious or not! Spirituality is about understanding and exploring your higher purpose, your interconnectedness to all of creation, and living authentically. It is my goal to help you feel inspired and fulfilled.

I do this by asking questions, giving suggestions, and then helping develop ways of marking progress and providing accountability. You don't have to believe the same way I, or anyone else, does. The coaching is centered around your needs and beliefs. I can't do the work for you, but I can help you with motivation and seeing things from a new perspective. Contact me now to schedule a free 15 minute initial consultation.

# A Restraining Order Due To Religion

While scrolling on TikTok I came across a rather concerning video with a woman claiming her neighbour took out a restraining order on her, because she's Wiccan. This stuck with me because, in the past few years, the world has become a more safe place for Wiccans, Pagans, and the like. While we do catch some flack now and then for our practice and beliefs, it's far better than even 10 years ago, so I was struck by this video.

Of course, I seem to have an issue keeping my nose to myself, so I had to interview her for the magazine. Note that personal information will be withheld, save for her user name.

When talking to shipwreckshark, hereby known as Shark, the first thing you notice is her warm personality. She's completely sociable, easy to talk to, and kind. Shark does not come off as the kind of person to start drama or enjoy conflict.

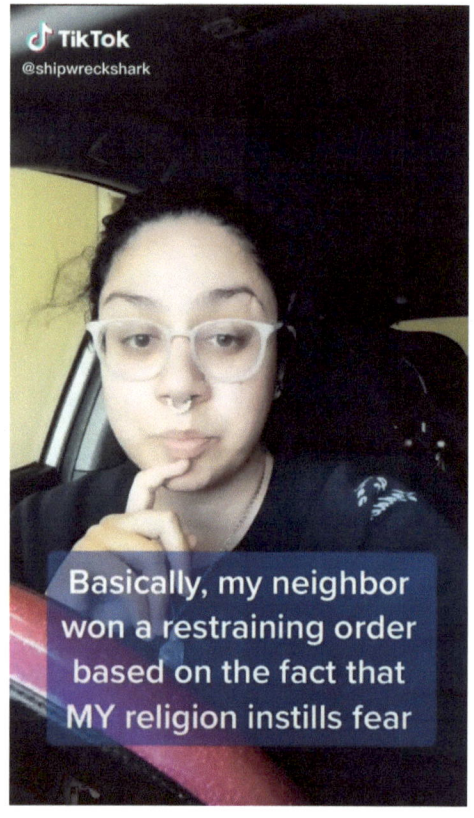

She lives in Alaska on base, as her husband is in the military. She lives with him and her young son. She is Wiccan and Puerto Rican and is studying to be an EMT with a 4.0 average in school. By all means, she is the ideal American, yet she found herself at the end of a restraining order based on bigotry.

So what happened? What lead to this? Shark and the neighbour originally started as friends but there were warning signs that the neighbour wasn't what she seemed from the start. Now everyone has at least one witch aesthetic thing, and Shark is no different. She had a Ouija board door mat which was the first thing that made the neighbour seemed uneasy about. Shark claims she's had a pride flag on the outside of her house so she was taken by surprise when the mat was a point of contention.

Alaska is a rather conservative state and Shark claims that the state can be rather unfriendly to both the Native and spiritual communities, so she accepted that the neighbour would likely be uncomfortable with her path, but nothing would prepare her for how the neighbour would act.

From the get-go, the neighbour would be uncomfortable around her house if so much as a tarot deck was out, so she began packing the more notable items away if the neighbour was coming over. That being said, she seemed interested, Shark commented about how the neighbour would ask questions about her beliefs, but no matter what she said, the neighbour would comment about how 'scary' it was.

Shark is a Wiccan and doesn't use magic to harm anyone, not that she could if she wanted to, given the Wiccan Rede which states to harm none and preaches the Rule Of Three. It was enough to make Shark uncomfortable and anyone reading can already see some red flags.

She would begin to show some toxic traits as Shark's husband went through a mental health crisis. Shark supported him through it, as a good partner should. The neighbour seemed to take offence to Shark's approach. Shark alleges that through her husband's difficulties the neighbour was urging her to leave him. The neighbour continued to keep trying to push her way into Shark's life and situation and it came to the point where she had to set up boundaries and tell her that she was no longer comfortable with her actions and that they couldn't be friends any more more.

The neighbour took this setting of boundaries personally and began saying that Shark implied that she hexes everyone she doesn't like.

Eventually, Shark's husband's situation improved and she rekindled her friendship with the neighbour. Yule comes and she has the neighbour over and things seemingly go better as the neighbour doesn't comment on her décor ( a hung pentacle with antlers and holly). A few weeks later Shark asked her neighbour if she would babysit her son as she had mentioned she had experience babysitting. The neighbour refused to do it in Shark's house as apparently, her house made the neighbour uncomfortable. It was clear she was on her best behaviour on Yule and she didn't plan on continuing to pretend any more.

The neighbour continued to push to have the kid at her house to the point where Shark began to get nervous, which caused the neighbour to take offence and begin her toxic antics again. Shark decided enough was enough and it became clear they could not be friends any more, despite her attempts.

This is where the neighbour becomes unhinged. She seemed to take Shark's setting of boundaries and not putting up with her toxicity as a personal slight and began a campaign of slander against Shark.

A shortened list of the accusations flung against Shark is as follows: tampering with her car in the middle of winter, smoking weed inside the house (note that marijuana is legal in Alaska, and she never had anything on base or smoked on base.), having and holding drugs on base, walking down the stairs in her home and slamming on the connected wall to disturb the neighbour.

Attached are images submitted by Shark. We have permission to share images from the report that she received. All names are censored to protect the identities of people involved

This went on for about a month before Shark confronted her. The neighbour would begin calling the cops on her numerous times. She noted that the neighbour herself had a smell of weed to her and she felt like she was trying to set her up as part of her little vendetta.

They ended up needing to talk to the military housing company because the neighbour ended up filing a complaint. This in itself is aggravating as Shark had filed a complaint against the neighbour when she began this over a month before, but was ignored.

Shark brought up the neighbour's anti-pagan stance and was ignored. The two left with nothing being done.

Two days later, Shark was woken by the police knocking at her door. Given the stress of her life mixed with the fact that her husband was away on training, this triggered a panic attack. She had assumed the police were there to tell her that her husband was hurt. Luckily when he heard about the incident and talked to the police, it was more of a formality than anything.

This neighbour apparently has a history of being somewhat of a Karen and has harassed and made enemies of many of the people she's met in her life.

The police eventually came back when she was calmer and explained why they were there. Shark had a cinnamon broom attached to her fence in her yard. Cinnamon brooms can be used to "sweep away" obstacles or negativity of people that were brought into your home. Seems like exactly the kind of thing a woman in her position would need, frankly.

Attached to the broom was a spell charm protected by a zip-lock bag with the words "Blessed Be" on it to protect from the constant rainstorms they were dealing with. The neighbour called the cops because she got the idea in her head that the bag had her name in it and it was a hex or curse against her.

The neighbour took it upon herself to bring her to court to get a restraining order on her shortly after. This is where things get... tricky. It is no secret that the military is usually pretty conservative, on top of the fact that she lives in a very conservative state, as she mentioned earlier.

Not only was the neighbour awarded the restraining order against Shark, but the judge also said that Shark's "religion can instill fear". The neighbour had a lawyer and Shark, as a mother and student did not so there wasn't a lot she could do aside from just dealing with it.

So to recap: an angry ex-friend who tried to get her [Shark] to leave her husband when he went through a mental health crisis harassed and lied and wasted police and military resources to get back at Shark for not putting up with her toxic and domineering attitude. The military refused to take Shark, the Puerto Rican Wiccan's harassment complaint, yet dealt with the white Christian's complaint quickly despite the obvious lies. Despite the right to religious freedom on which the United States Of America is founded on, a judge looked her in the eyes and told her that because of her religion, people fear her to the point where restraining orders are an appropriate course of action.

It baffles the mind to think about the hypocrisy of this situation. This is not something that would ever happen if we turned the tables. You would not see months of harassment, fake phone calls to the police, and restraining orders because you saw a bible once at your friend's house, and then she hung a cross outside. Why is it that we bend over backward to cater to Christians whenever we can, from removing their kids from sex ed to literally forming the bank and work cycles of the country around their practices and religion but all a non-Christian has to do to get BROUGHT TO ACTUAL COURT is to hang a good luck charm?

Shark is preparing to fight back however, she will be appealing and doing whatever she can to make this right. She is not laying down and taking this crap. She is building her appeal, but no longer feels safe in her own home. Her husband leaves again soon and she doesn't leave the house without her family or friends on video call as now the neighbour has installed cameras focused on her cars to watch her. She fears that the moment her husband leaves, the neighbour will begin again, as she has been doing this when her husband is gone.

I wish there was a resolution to the situation, but unfortunately, this has only just begun. Who knows how long the appeal will take or if she will even win the appeal. Shark makes it very clear that she does not think that this sort of thing would happen in other states, and I'd have to agree.

*-Desirée Goulden*

## Metaphysical Crossword Answers!

1- Thor
2- Odin
3- Oracle
4- Deosil
5- Zeus
6- Wicca
7- Minotaur
8- Hellenismos
9- Futharkn
10- Pagan
11- Norse

## Olympian Crossworsd Answers!

1- Demeter
2- Hemes
3- Athena
4- Zeus
5- Aphrodite
6- Hestia
7- Apollo
8- Hephaestus
9- Dionysus
10- Hera
11- Poseidon
12- Artemis

## Olympian Crossworsd Answers!

1- malachite
2- rhodochrosite
3- fluorite
4- citrine
5- garnet
6- quartz
7- celestite
8- pyrite
9- amethyst
10- azurite

Have news?

Have a story to share or a cause to fight for?

Let us know!

Email us at TalesOTheGods@gmail.com and we will cover your story!

Enjoyed this edition? Rate us on GoodReads.com or Amazon!
Keep an eye on TalesOfTheGods.com or the Practical Witchcraft group for updates on free giveaways like our Litha & Pride edition!

Photo Credits

Owen Lee Heavenhill - Cover, pg 2, 4, 5

Soulful Stock - pg 6

Roberto Barbara - pg 8

Paulina H - 12

Joshua Rawson Harris - pg 14

www.ingramcontent.com/pod-product-compliance
Lightning Source LLC
Chambersburg PA
CBHW042255100526
44589CB00002B/22